Trusting God in Times of Adversity

KAY ARTHUR
PETE DE LACY

D0962690

HARVEST HOUSE™ PUBLISHERS

EUGENE, OREGON

All Scripture quotations in this book are taken from the New American Standard Bible®, © 1960, 1962, 1963, 1968, 1971, 1972, 1973, 1975, 1977, 1995 by The Lockman Foundation. Used by permission.

Cover by Koechel Peterson & Associates, Minneapolis, Minnesota

The New Inductive Study Series
TRUSTING GOD IN TIMES OF ADVERSITY
Copyright © 2003 by Precept Ministries International
Published by Harvest House Publishers
Eugene, Oregon 97402
www.harvesthousepublishers.com

Library of Congress Cataloging-in-Publication Data
Arthur, Kay, 1933-
    Trusting God in times of adversity / Kay Arthur and Pete De Lacy.
        p. cm. — (New inductive study series)
    ISBN-13: 978-0-7369-1268-6
    ISBN-10: 0-7369-1268-1
    1. Bible. O.T. Job — Textbooks.   I. De Lacy, Pete.   II. Title.
BS1415.55.A78 2003
223'.1'0071—dc21   2003003784

Printed in the United States of America

08 09 10 11 12 13 14 / BP-MS / 13 12 11 10 9 8 7 6 5

CONTENTS

HOW TO GET STARTED...

Reading directions is sometimes difficult and hardly ever enjoyable! Most often you just want to get started. Only if all else fails will you read the instructions. We understand, but please don't approach this study that way. These brief instructions are a vital part of getting started on the right foot! These few pages will help you immensely.

FIRST

As you study Job, you will need four things in addition to this book:

1. A Bible that you are willing to mark in. The marking is essential. An ideal Bible for this purpose is *The New Inductive Study Bible (NISB)*. The *NISB* is in a single-column text format with large, easy-to-read type, which is ideal for marking. The margins of the text are wide and blank for note taking.

The *NISB* also has instructions for studying each book of the Bible, but it does not contain any commentary on the text, nor is it compiled from any theological stance. Its purpose is to teach you how to discern truth for yourself through the inductive method of study. (The various charts and maps that you will find in this study guide are taken from the *NISB*.)

Whatever Bible you use, just know you will need to mark in it, which brings us to the second item you will need...

2. A fine-point, four-color ballpoint pen or various colored fine-point pens that you can use to write in your Bible. Office supply stores should have these.

3. Colored pencils or an eight-color leaded Pentel pencil.

4. A composition book or a notebook for working on your assignments or recording your insights.

SECOND

1. As you study Job, you will be given specific instructions for each day's study. These should take you between 20 and 30 minutes a day, but if you desire to spend more time than this, you will increase your intimacy with the Word of God and the God of the Word.

If you are doing this study within the framework of a class and you find the lessons too heavy, then simply do what you can. To do a little is better than to do nothing. Don't be an all-or-nothing person when it comes to Bible study.

Remember, any time you get into the Word of God, you enter into more intensive warfare with the devil (our enemy). Why? Every piece of the Christian's armor is related to the Word of God. And our one and only offensive weapon is the sword of the Spirit, which is the Word of God. The enemy wants you to have a dull sword. Don't cooperate! You don't have to!

2. As you read each chapter, train yourself to ask the "5 W's and an H": who, what, when, where, why, and how. Asking questions like these helps you see exactly what the Word of God is saying. When you interrogate the text with the 5 W's and an H, you ask questions like these:

a. **What** is the chapter about?

b. **Who** are the main characters?

c. **When** does this event or teaching take place?

d. **Where** does this happen?

e. **Why** is this being done or said?

f. **How** did it happen?

3. The "when" of events or teachings is very important and should be marked in an easily recognizable way in your Bible. You could mark it with a clock (like the one shown here) ⏰ in the margin of your Bible beside the verse where the time phrase occurs. You may want to underline or color the references to time in one specific color.

4. You will be given certain key words to mark throughout the book of Job. This is the purpose of the colored pencils and the colored pens. If you will develop the habit of marking your Bible in this way, you will find it will make a significant difference in the effectiveness of your study and in how much you remember.

A **key word** is an important word that is used by the author repeatedly in order to convey his message to his reader. Certain key words will show up throughout the book; others will be concentrated in specific chapters or segments of the book. When you mark a key word, you should also mark its synonyms (words that mean the same thing in the context) and any pronouns (*he, his, she, her, it, we, they, us, our, you, their, them*) in the same way you have marked the key word. We will give you suggestions for ways to mark key words in your daily assignments.

Marking words for easy identification can be done by colors or symbols or a combination of colors and symbols. However, colors are easier to distinguish than symbols. When we use symbols, we keep them very simple. For example, you could color *repent* yellow but put a red diagram like this over it repent because it indicates a change of mind.

When marking key words, mark them in a way that is easy for you to remember.

If you devise a color-coding system for marking key words throughout your Bible, then when you look at the pages of your Bible, you will see instantly where a key word is used.

You might want to make yourself a bookmark listing the words you want to mark along with their colors and/or symbols.

5. A chart called JOB AT A GLANCE is located at the end of your study guide. As you complete your study of each chapter, record the main theme of that chapter under the appropriate chapter number. The main theme of a chapter is what the chapter deals with the most. It may be an event or a particular subject or teaching. Usually in a historical or biographical book, the chapter themes center on events.

If you will fill out the JOB AT A GLANCE chart as you progress through the study, you will have a complete synopsis of the book when you are finished. If you have a *New Inductive Study Bible,* you will find the same chart in your Bible (pages 874–75). If you record your chapter themes there, you'll have them for a ready reference.

6. Always begin your study with prayer. As you do your part to handle the Word of God accurately, you must remember that the Bible is a divinely inspired book. The words that you are reading are truth, given to you by God so you can know Him and His ways more intimately. These truths are divinely revealed.

> For to us God revealed them through the Spirit;
> for the Spirit searches all things, even the depths of

God. For who among men knows the thoughts of
a man except the spirit of the man which is in him?
Even so the thoughts of God no one knows except
the Spirit of God (1 Corinthians 2:10-11).

Therefore ask God to reveal His truth to you as He
leads and guides you into all truth. He will, if you will ask.

7. Each day when you finish your lesson, meditate on
what you saw. Ask your heavenly Father how you should
live in light of the truths you have just studied. At times,
depending on how God has spoken to you through His
Word, you might even want to record these "Lessons for
Life" in the margin of your Bible next to the text you have
studied. Simply put "LFL" in the margin of your Bible, and
then, as briefly as possible, record the lesson for life that
you want to remember.

THIRD

This study is set up so that you have an assignment for
every day of the week—so that you are in the Word daily.
If you work through your study in this way, you will find it
more profitable than doing a week's study in one sitting.
Pacing yourself this way allows time for thinking through
what you learn on a daily basis!

The seventh day of each week differs from the other six
days. The seventh day is designed to aid group discussion;
however, it's also profitable if you are studying this book
individually.

The "seventh" day is whatever day in the week you
choose to finish your week's study. On this day, you will
find a verse or two for you to memorize and STORE IN YOUR
HEART. Then there is a passage to READ AND DISCUSS. This
will help you focus on a major truth or major truths
covered in your study that week.

To assist those using the material in a Sunday school class or a group Bible study, there are QUESTIONS FOR DISCUSSION OR INDIVIDUAL STUDY. Even if you are not doing this study with anyone else, it would be good for you to answer these questions.

If you are in a group, be sure every member of the class, including the teacher, supports his or her answers and insights from the Bible text itself. Then you will be handling the Word of God accurately. As you learn to see what the text says and compare Scripture with Scripture, the Bible explains itself.

Always examine your insights by carefully observing the text to see what it *says*. Then, before you decide what the passage of Scripture *means*, make sure that you interpret it in the light of its context. Scripture will never contradict Scripture. If it ever seems to contradict the rest of the Word of God, you can be certain that something is being taken out of context. If you come to a passage that is difficult to understand, reserve your interpretations for a time when you can study the passage in greater depth.

The purpose of the THOUGHT FOR THE WEEK is to share with you what we consider to be an important element in your week of study. We have included it for your evaluation and, hopefully, for your edification. This section will help you see how to walk in light of what you learned.

Books in The New Inductive Study Series are survey courses. If you want to do a more in-depth study of a particular book of the Bible, we suggest you do a Precept Upon Precept Bible study course on that book. You may obtain more information on these courses by contacting Precept Ministries International at 800-763-8280, visiting our website at www.precept.org, or filling out and mailing the response card in the back of this book.

JOB

FINDING GOD
IN THE DARKNESS

∾∾∾∾

"Your children are dead!" These words pierce the heart with a pain that has no equal. "Your house has burned down!" The pain is less, but *What do I do now that I've lost everything I owned? Why did this happen? No, no...it can't be true!* Anger, grief, denial—these are typical reactions. How do we handle such losses?

The book of Job can help us face life's greatest pains and losses. As it begins, Job has everything he could ask for—family, friends, health, great material wealth, and a strong faith in God. Then in one day he lost his possessions, his servants, and even his children. Soon after that, he lost his health. Had God abandoned him? Was He punishing him for sin? Was He being fair, just, and righteous—or just cruel, toying with a man for His own pleasure? Did God really love Job? How could He, allowing such terrible circumstances as these?

Job's friends and his wife attached the blame to Job. They could not fault God for any of the tragic disasters that occurred, nor could they see Job's unwavering devotion, steadfast faith, and complete commitment. That left Job and Job alone to blame. Surely he was hiding something, some specific sin that brought these judgments on him.

But Job himself saw a sovereign God behind the scenes and believed, trusting Him in spite of what happened. He was quite alone in this faith because his family and friends, like many today, equated God's love and favor with physical prosperity. They could not see a gracious, sovereign God in the darkness Job was facing—only a disobedient man.

This is precisely what Satan wants to do—to blind us so we can't find God in the impossible experiences of life. He wants us to abandon faith and curse God— the only reasonable product of a *Why?* with no answer. But the book of Job teaches us to rise above excruciating trials by bowing before the Living God. If we can keep faith after we've lost everything else, God will ultimately bless us in ways that will bring praise to our lips and glory to Him.

HOLDING FAST YOUR INTEGRITY

When you squeeze olives in an olive press, what oozes out? Olive oil, of course! Why? Because you pressed olives. You can't get grape juice by pressing olives or olive oil by pressing grapes. What comes out under pressure reveals what we really are. What happens when the pressure is on in our lives? What oozes out? Whatever we are made of.

One of the first things we learn about Job is that he was a man under extreme pressure who experienced unparalleled personal disaster. His responses reveal what he really was.

DAY ONE

No one knows for sure when the book of Job was written or when the events took place. Some believe Job lived at the time of Abraham and that Moses either found or wrote the book. Others think it was written at the time of Solomon or later. Even *where* Job lived is uncertain. But dates, location, and even authorship are not crucial to our understanding of the timeless truths in this book. We need to focus only on Job's character—how he responds to overwhelming circumstances and what he believes about the character of God in the midst of these circumstances.

These are the things that will help us maintain integrity when life's pressures seem impossible to bear.

Read Job 1 today, marking every reference to *God*. You might want to use the color yellow because God is light, or a triangle, which reminds us that God is three in one.

On another sheet of paper, make a list of what you learn about God. You might want to get a spiral notebook to keep the notes you make from your studies. Or you could simply put a triangle in the margin of your Bible and there record anything you learn about God.

Seeking to understand all we can about God is essential when we study the Bible because the Bible is God's written revelation of Himself to us. Be sure to note God's character, ways, and sovereignty over history in general and over Satan, man, and nature in particular.

DAY TWO

Today read Job 1 again. As you do, mark every reference to *Satan* with a red pitchfork. Although there is no biblical basis for the color red or the pitchfork, it's an image that has stuck with Western culture since the Middle Ages.

The word *Satan* means adversary. As in war, learning in advance all you can about opponents can help you know how they operate and what offensive and defensive countermeasures to make to gain advantages. By the time the New Testament authors composed their writings, the church had a great deal of biblical information about the devil. Consequently, Paul could say that we're not ignorant of his tactics (2 Corinthians 2:11). So list in your notebook all you learn about Satan from this chapter. Be sure to note his character, tactics, and the limits God places on his power.

DAY THREE

Read Job 1 again today. This time, mark every reference to *Job* (you choose the symbol and color).

Make a list of what you learn about Job—how he is described and what happens to him.

DAY FOUR

Read through Job 1 again and mark the words *sin* and *sinned.* Though the word *sin* does not appear many times, it's central to the message of this book. In fact, the main controversy in Job is the relationship between sin and suffering.

In coming chapters, you will see *iniquity* and *transgression* used as synonyms for *sin.* Mark these words the same way.

Also mark *sons of God*[1] in a distinctive way. Note who is included in this class of creatures.

Make a bookmark with these words and the respective markings for each one. This will help you to be consistent throughout Job and also to remember what key term you're marking and how you will mark each one. Add to this bookmark as you go through Job, and refer to it in your daily study.

DAY FIVE

Perhaps the greatest conflict in Scripture is between God and Satan. Some references outside the book of Job will help us to understand this conflict better.

One of the first things to notice is that "the sons of God" came to present themselves before the Lord with Satan among them. Let's look at some scriptures that help identify these "sons of God" and explain why Satan is among them. Read Job 38:4-7; Isaiah 14:12-14; and Ezekiel 28:12-17. Then read Genesis 3:1-15 and Revelation 20:2.

DAY SIX

Make a short outline of this chapter to help you see the flow of events.

When we study a book of the Bible, we need to identify the main theme of each chapter. As for historical books and this book of poetic narrative, recording the main events, profound statements from characters, and wonderful truths about God will help you remember what each chapter is about. Record the theme of Job chapter 1 on JOB AT A GLANCE on pages 97–98.

DAY SEVEN

 Store in your heart: Job 1:21.

Read and discuss: Job 1; 38:4-7; Isaiah 14:12-14; Ezekiel 28:12-17.

QUESTIONS FOR DISCUSSION OR INDIVIDUAL STUDY

∾ Discuss Job's situation at the beginning. What family did he have? What possessions? What was Job's relationship to God with respect to his family?

∽ What did you learn about Satan and his relationship to God? Where can Satan go? What can he do? What can he not do?

∽ From what you observed, whose adversary is Satan? God's? Man's? Explain your answer using Job 1.

∽ Review what Satan did to Job. What did Job lose? How did he lose it?

∽ What do these events teach you about God's power over man, nature, and Satan? What did you learn about Satan's power over man and nature? How do they relate?

∽ What does Satan believe about why people obey God? Can you tell from Job's reaction in these first two chapters whether Satan is right or wrong?

∽ Why does God permit Satan to afflict Job? What is His purpose? How far will He let Satan go? Does God agree or does He disagree with Satan's accusation that Job's faith is based on his prosperity?

∽ Describe Job's relationship to God. How do Job's actions in this chapter reflect on God's opinion of Job?

∽ How has what you learned about Satan and God affected your understanding of their relationship to each other? What changes would this make in your attitude toward your circumstances?

∽ What questions come to mind that are not answered in this chapter? (Remember, we have 12 more weeks of study in Job to address questions we don't have answers for now.)

THOUGHT FOR THE WEEK

Although most people have not read the book of Job, many know one thing about the main character because of a common idiom given as a compliment—"He has the patience of Job"—echoing James 5:11. The compliment, however, emphasizes only one of Job's spiritual qualities. Job was not only patient in his circumstances—but also faithful to God and God's revealed truth. The book focuses on *patient faith,* not a bare patience an unbeliever might have. True, he waited for God, but he *waited believing* in a sovereignty that would vindicate him "at the last" (Job 19:25). He did not relax this doctrine for a moment (see Week 7, Day 7).

In spite of the absolutely horrible set of calamities that occurred—the loss of possessions and children—Job did not sin or blame God. How many of us have this kind of faith? How do we react when we lose possessions or family members? Does our relationship to God include patient faith?

We might know how we *should* act and think, based on what God's Word says. But the burning question in circumstances like these remains: "Why? Why, God?" Job never gets an answer. The first two chapters show us the reason Job suffers, but *Job* knows nothing about Satan provoking God into testing his integrity and letting the devil do the afflicting. Job doesn't know that this is God's way of proving to Satan that faith exists independent of worldly prosperity and endures in times of loss. Nor does Job know that God knows he will not fail the tests.

But we must learn a valuable lesson. The book of Job never answers the question, "Why do we suffer?" The way to cope with suffering is not to find out the immediate cause but to find out who God is. A deep, personal knowledge of God, our Creator, Sustainer, and Redeemer is what we need to handle the stress of suffering. We need a relationship with God that enables us to endure suffering without losing faith, without cursing God, and without blaspheming God's name in actions and words.

We must learn that trials help us grow in faith. James wrote about this radical perspective:

> Consider it all joy, my brethren, when you encounter various trials, knowing that the testing of your faith produces endurance. And let endurance have its perfect result, so that you may be perfect and complete, lacking in nothing (James 1:2-4).

SHALL WE ACCEPT GOOD FROM GOD AND NOT ADVERSITY?

∾∾∾∾

Most of us complain about daily trials we suffer. Job, on the other hand, suffered unimaginable losses. His relationship to God was strong, but was it strong enough? Would he be able to endure what God allowed next? And why would God do such a thing?

DAY ONE

Read Job 2 today, marking every reference to *God* as you did last week (refer to your bookmark for the symbol and color). Then add to your list from chapter 1 all that you learn in chapter 2 about God. Be sure to note His power.

DAY TWO

Today, read Job 2 again and mark every reference to *Job*. Use the same marking system you recorded on your bookmark last week. As you have done before, list what you learn about Job's responses to circumstances and especially his reaction to affliction and to his wife's comments.

DAY THREE

Read through Job 2 one more time today, marking *sin* and *sons of God*² as you did in Job 1. Also mark the words *integrity* and *curse*. Choose a symbol and color for each word and add these to your bookmark. You won't find these words often in this chapter, but they are important throughout the rest of the book.

When you mark words and make lists, take a moment to ask the "5 W's and an H" questions. For example, Who sinned (or didn't sin)? Who said to curse? Why? Training yourself to read this way helps you interact with the text and become a more careful reader.

DAY FOUR

Satan appeared in Job 1. We marked *Satan* in our text, listed things we learned, and looked at some Old Testament scriptures that taught us some things about who he is and where he came from. This kind of information about him is necessary for understanding Job. Read Job 2 again, mark *Satan*, and add what you learn to the list you started last week.

DAY FIVE

Last week we looked at Old Testament scriptures about Satan to help us understand his relationships with God and Job. This week, we'll look at some New Testament scriptures to help us understand his relationship to us today.

Read Matthew 4:1-11; Luke 22:31-32; Acts 26:16-18; 2 Corinthians 11:14; Ephesians 6:11; 1 Timothy 3:6-7; 5:15; Hebrews 2:14; James 4:7; and 1 Peter 5:8.

If you list what you learn about Satan from these verses, you will see that he is Jesus' adversary and therefore ours. In these first two chapters, you will begin to see how motivated Satan is to do evil and to afflict Job—and us. He is even willing to provoke *God* into letting him do evil!

DAY SIX

Again this week, make a short outline of this chapter to help you see the flow of events. This will help you understand the remaining chapters.

Record the theme of Job 2 on JOB AT A GLANCE.

DAY SEVEN

Store in your heart: Job 2:10.

Read and discuss: Job 2 and the cross-references about Satan.

QUESTIONS FOR DISCUSSION OR INDIVIDUAL STUDY

∾ What questions does God ask Satan, and what are Satan's responses? Are they the same?

∾ Notice what God says in His second question to Satan. What has happened that would cause God to add the last part about His integrity?

∾ How did Satan provoke God further? From Job 1 and God's response in Job 2:3, why do you think Satan pressed God more?

∾ From God's response this time, do you learn anything new about God's power over man and Satan or Satan's power over man? Is there an interrelationship?

∾ What do we learn in Job 2 about Satan's opinion of why people obey God? Does Job prove Satan right or wrong?

∾ As things get worse for Job, does his relationship to God change? Is God's confidence in Job justified?

∾ Who comes to help Job? What are their names, and what do they do when they arrive? In the coming weeks of study, we'll hear much from these friends. What would you expect from someone who came to comfort you when you had troubles like Job's?

∾ What lessons can you draw from Job 2 about comforting friends? What changes do you need to make in how you comfort friends?

∾ Summarize the flow of thought from these first two chapters. Go over the events and what you learn about God, Satan, and Job. From God's description of Job, what do you anticipate about Job in the remaining chapters?

THOUGHT FOR THE WEEK

The preacher's words shocked me: "You don't have to believe Satan is real. The family of God has room for all of us."

I saw my wife grip the edge of her chair and her knuckles turn white. How could any preacher let people think Satan is not real? If they assume he's simply a myth, they will never know how to deal with him. They will be unaware of his schemes and unprepared for his attacks.

The preacher's viewpoint makes a mockery out of Jesus' temptation in the wilderness. Perhaps Jesus isn't real either. If that's so, then salvation, resurrection, and hope for a life better than this one are all gone. What a gloomy future. Life is hard and then you die.

The Bible tells us to be on the lookout for the devil, to wear armor, and to stand firm. He is real, and he's coming for you. But God is in control. Ultimately, Satan will be defeated and cast into the lake of fire, where he will undergo torment forever. His judgment is sure. In this life, we will have tribulation as the "ruler of the world" seeks whom he may devour, but his judgment and defeat have already been accomplished by the cross of Christ, as the apostle John well points out (John 12:31).

Oh, that you would understand that Eve chose to sin because Satan tempted her, and this enemy of mankind will continue to tempt us right up to his final defeat! Be on the lookout! Be ready!

I Wish I Had Never Been Born!

Have you ever had this wish? Job certainly had good cause: his children were dead, his servants were dead, his herds and flocks were either dead or stolen, and now he was afflicted with an agonizing disease. His wife advised him to curse God and die. His friends came to sit with him, but they did not help. Most of us can only imagine how Job's circumstances made him feel. At such points in life, we might wish we had never been born.

How can anyone cope with such prolonged disaster? Why do such things happen? Even if Job had known what we know from the prologue—God's dialogue with Satan—would he have been able to cope any better? Does that information help us cope better with our own sufferings?

DAY ONE

Read Job 3, marking all references to key words and phrases as you have done previously. Add the word *death* to your bookmark, and mark synonyms like *die, kill, expire, perish, grave,* etc. You may want to draw a tombstone around or an X on these words. Feel free to invent your own symbols that help you identify these key words.

When you are done marking, note what Job cursed and what he wishes for. Then record the theme of Job 3 on JOB AT A GLANCE.

DAY TWO

Read and mark Job 4 today. You will note that one of Job's three friends who have come to visit speaks to him. (Do you remember the arrival of his friends from studying chapter 2?) Read Job 2:11 and note why they came to be with Job. Then, as you read Job 4, note who is speaking and underline or highlight any important phrases that reflect the speaker's opinion of Job. Also watch for his explanation of why these things have happened to Job.

Add *wisdom* and *just* (and its synonym *righteous*) to your bookmark. Although these words are used infrequently, they are still key to the whole book. As before, mark synonyms.

As you read and mark key words and phrases, observe what the text says about

∾ man and God

∾ what God expects from man and what He does not expect

∾ nature

∾ physical life and death

∾ how to deal with those in pain

Don't forget to write the main subject or theme of chapter 4 on JOB AT A GLANCE. The primary complaints or responses of Job in chapters 4–31 will help you determine the themes of those chapters.

DAY THREE

Today, read Job 5, which concludes Eliphaz' discourse. Mark as you did yesterday, again observing the five things listed in Day Two.

Remember to record the theme of chapter 5 on JOB AT A GLANCE. Job's friends' explanations for Job's condition can also help you determine the themes of chapters 4–37.

DAY FOUR

Today read Job 6, Job's response to Eliphaz. Mark as you did yesterday, observing the five things listed in Day Two. Think about what Eliphaz says to explain Job's situation. How does Job respond to Eliphaz?

Remember to record the theme of Job 6 on JOB AT A GLANCE.

DAY FIVE

Read Job 7 today, marking as you have done before. Job 7 concludes Job's response to Eliphaz. Job 6 and 7 together make up his complete response. If you need to, read these two chapters together.

Record the theme of Job 7 on JOB AT A GLANCE.

DAY SIX

Chapters 4–7 make up the first part of a cycle of discourse between Job and his friends. In Job 4–14, Job hears from each of his three friends and then responds.

Each friend has an explanation for his condition, and Job has a response for each of them. In Job 4–7, we have Eliphaz' appraisal and Job's response. Jump ahead to Job 42:7 to get a quick, one-line summary of what God thinks of Eliphaz' opinions.

In light of Job 42:7, reread Job 4–7 and be sure you can see what Eliphaz has said that is true and what he has said that misrepresents God. What you can't see now should be clear by the end of the book so hang in there!

DAY SEVEN

Store in your heart: Job 5:17.
Read and discuss: Job 3:1-3; 4:1-11; 5:6-7,17; 6:24-30; 7:20-21.

QUESTIONS FOR DISCUSSION OR INDIVIDUAL STUDY

∞ How does Job react to his circumstances in chapter 3? Are his words directed at God or at himself? Review what chapters 1 and 2 say Job did regarding God.

∞ Is Job asking about the *who, what, when, where, why,* or *how* of his circumstances? Which one is his main question?

∞ What contrast does Eliphaz make in Job 4:1-6? What point is he making to Job?

∞ In Job 4:7-11, what does Eliphaz say is the cause of Job's afflictions?

∞ How does Eliphaz justify his claim? Where does he get his ideas? Are these safe sources of information, considering Job 42:7? Should we base our knowledge of God on these things?

- According to Eliphaz' statement in 5:7, for what is a man born? How does this relate to Job's lament in Job 3?

- To whom would Eliphaz turn? Is any part of his appraisal of God correct?

- According to what we know from Job 1–2 about the cause of Job's afflictions, is Eliphaz correct in Job 5:17 when he says Job is being disciplined?

- Should we despise discipline from the Lord? Read Proverbs 3:11-12.

- What does Job say in Job 6 about the advice he gets from Eliphaz?

- Does Job agree with Eliphaz that his affliction is the result of some specific sin he is covering up? Use Job 7 to support your answer.

THOUGHT FOR THE WEEK

Eliphaz is clearly Job's friend. Hearing about Job's affliction, he has come to sit in silence, mourning with Job for the loss of Job's family, servants, and livestock, as well as the terrible disease that racks Job's body. As a friend, he has given Job counsel, but the counsel is flawed because it is not based on the Word of God. Instead, it is based on Eliphaz' general life experiences and on a very questionable, ambiguous vision he received one night.

Eliphaz has told Job that the innocent do not suffer. His counsel is that Job's sufferings are direct evidence that Job has committed some sin and that Job must repent for that sin before God will relent from this affliction. Eliphaz has told Job that God would be unjust to afflict Job unless Job was guilty of some specific unconfessed sin, and that God is just. In Eliphaz' understanding of God, Job could not be afflicted for any reason other than God's just judgment of Job's sin. We know from Job 1–2 that Eliphaz is wrong.

To rise above his circumstances and maintain faith in the midst of this great trial, Job needs counsel that accurately explains God's relationship with him. Although we may know the Scriptures from prior study, during times of extreme anguish we may need someone to explain them to us, or if we have the strength, we can turn to them directly. The only true knowledge and counsel is God's Word; no other counsel will work. Friends may have experiences similar to ours, and they may have come through severe trials, but the one true God has given one clear revelation of Himself; the Word of God. Counsel, comfort, support, and wisdom from those who have been through similar trials can help sustain us during our trials, and we must not discount this ministry, but our friends must give an accurate representation of God according to His Word.

You may have heard the common saying, "Experience is the best teacher." It is designed to motivate us to apply theories we learn from classrooms or textbooks. But this statement is not strictly true. We don't always draw the correct lesson from an experience. Eliphaz' experiences had not given Him a correct understanding of God.

The best teacher about God is God's own revelation to us in His inerrant Word. That truth not only informs us about God and His ways but also has supernatural power to judge the thoughts and intentions of our hearts (Hebrews 4:12), showing us where we might be wrong. It has power to teach, reprove, correct, and train in righteousness (2 Timothy 3:16).

You and I might never walk through experiences like Job's, but God's Word shows us God's character and the way we should respond to Him when we have trials. Whatever comfort we have from friends in times of trial is measured the same way as the comfort of Job's friends: Is it true according to God's Word?

Praise God for family and friends who bring godly counsel and comfort to us in time of need. But praise God, too, for giving us His Word and His Holy Spirit, Who indwells believers and brings into memory what Jesus has taught (John 14:26).

Turn to Him, run to God, hold on to His Word. Let it wash over you, lift you, and sustain you in your trials!

DOES GOD AFFLICT THE GUILTLESS?

Perhaps you've wondered what you did to bring certain problems into your life. Job's friends make some interesting assumptions as they give him counsel. In Job 4 and 5, Eliphaz assumed that his private experiences and vision qualified him to answer Job. He also assumed that Job has sinned. Now Job's friend Bildad chimes in based on the same assumption Eliphaz holds—that specific suffering is the direct result of some specific sin. Job is suffering, and suffering comes because of sin; therefore, Job has sinned—he can't be guiltless. Conclusions are only as good as the premises that support them. Here, the false assumption that suffering comes *only* from sin leads to a false conclusion.

DAY ONE

Read Job 8, marking key words and noting the things that you have listed on your bookmark. Don't forget to record the theme of Job 8 on JOB AT A GLANCE. (Hint: Look for Bildad's main accusation against Job.)

DAY TWO

We need to thoroughly examine Bildad's thesis that suffering comes only from sin and is therefore strictly punitive. Legalism is pervasive and spiritually oppressive, so we must know whether this theory is right or wrong. Today let's look at some cross-references in the New Testament regarding suffering to see what God says. Read the following scriptures and then write in your notebook some summary bullets about the positive value suffering has in the life of believers: Romans 8:16-18; Colossians 1:24; 2 Thessalonians 1:3-8; 1 Peter 2:18-23; 3:14-17; 4:1-2,13-19; 5:8-10.

DAY THREE

Read Job 9 and mark it as you have the earlier chapters. This chapter begins Job's response to Bildad's accusations.

Don't forget to record the chapter theme on JOB AT A GLANCE.

DAY FOUR

Job has responded that God is sovereign. The Lord, he says, does as He wills, *but He destroys the guiltless and the wicked together.*

Is this right? How powerful is God? (See Numbers 11:23 and 2 Chronicles 20:6.) He's omnipotent, powerful enough to destroy anything He has created. But what about this idea of destroying the guiltless and the wicked *together*?

The polarity between Job and his friends is interesting. Job is convinced he's guiltless, so he concludes that God treats the innocent and the guilty alike. His friends, on the other hand, can't believe that God would do such an immoral thing. They're forced to conclude that Job is hiding some awful sin.

How do we resolve this tension? We know Job is not sinless because of dozens of Scriptures that tell us that man is universally depraved (Romans 3:10,23). Jesus Christ is the only exception. Even Job makes statements that imply that he's not *conscious* of any sins that would incur such awful judgments (see Job 7:20-21; 10:6; 13:23) and that the minor offenses he *has* committed have been forgiven (Job 14:16-17). Toward the end of the book, Job will confess that he wrongfully accused God of treating the guiltless and the guilty alike. But this comes later and does not relate to the sins that occurred prior to the afflictions he's enduring now.

God had boasted to Satan in the first chapter that Job was "blameless." How do we reconcile this with those Scriptures that tell us that every man is a sinner in thought, word, and deed? We have to differentiate blamelessness from sinlessness. Certainly when God told Satan that Job was blameless, He did not mean that He could not find any sin within the man over the course of his entire life. Rather, God was bringing into the open something He knew Satan had thought about and would agree to: He (Satan) could not fault Job. The devil admits this in effect when he assigns a cause to Job's blamelessness: "Have you not made a hedge about him?" By asserting a cause (prosperity), Satan was conceding the effect (blamelessness).

Given this clear difference between sinlessness and blamelessness, the options are not just two—either (1) Job is sinless (i.e., God Himself can't find fault) or (2) God is unjust. A third option is that Job has not done any specific sin to merit this specific suffering. This is clearly what chapters 1 and 2 teach, and this option is probably closest to Job's claim about himself. He was not likely to think of himself as *absolutely* sinless, but he did sincerely believe that he had done nothing *in particular* to deserve the particular afflictions handed to him. In this restricted sense, he was right and his friends were wrong.

DAY FIVE

Chapter 10 continues Job's response to Bildad. Read this chapter and continue to mark and note as you have before. Add *wicked* to your bookmark. Most chapters of the book of Job address this contrast between the righteous and the wicked and how they are treated. Mark all of the synonyms for *wicked* (like *godless*) as you come to them. Does Job address Bildad or God in this chapter? What does Job say to God in chapter 10 that echoes what he said in chapter 3?

DAY SIX

Outline the main points Bildad makes as he instructs Job and then Job's points in his response. Notice that Bildad does not comfort Job but instead rebukes him. Read 2 Corinthians 1:8-9 to see how the apostle Paul handles despair. Does Job understand this? Do you?

Remember to add the theme of Job 10 to JOB AT A GLANCE.

DAY SEVEN

Store in your heart: Job 8:3.

Read and discuss: Job 8:1-11,20-22; 9:1-10,19-24; 10:1-7.

QUESTIONS FOR DISCUSSION OR INDIVIDUAL STUDY

∾ Briefly summarize Bildad's discourse. What does he ask Job to consider?

∾ Do platitudes and proverbs provide effective answers to suffering? Why?

∾ What does Bildad say about the Lord?

∾ How does Job respond? What does he say about God?

∾ From Job's words about God, how does he see himself compared to God?

∾ What is the main point of Job 10? What does Job want to know?

∾ Has Job learned anything from these first two friends to help him answer the basic question about his terrible circumstances?

∾ Does Job seem to agree or to disagree with his friends? About everything or some things?

∾ Do you identify in any way with Job? Have you responded like Job to similar situations?

THOUGHT FOR THE WEEK

Eliphaz argued that Job's particular sufferings were a result of some specific sin because he believed suffering comes only upon the wicked. He used his own experiences and a vision to make his case. But Job remained steadfast in declaring that he had not committed a specific sin that caused these tragedies.

Bildad, too, tells Job that his suffering is a result of his sin, that if he would just stop complaining and confess, his suffering would end. To convince Job of this, he appeals to ancient proverbs and platitudes.

Job answers that even though he is innocent, God can fault him because He is all-powerful and can do whatever He wants. Job laments that God will destroy the innocent with the guilty. He knows God can rescue him but can't understand why He hasn't.

Job, of course, is despairing at this point, unable "to see the forest for the trees." The "tree" that blinds him is the limitation he places on the *purpose* of suffering—namely, to punish wicked people. The "forest" has more answers, but he can't see beyond the tree. At this point, for example, he seems to have lost sight of the fact that God sanctifies His people by fire (Zechariah 13:9; 1 Corinthians 3:15; 1 Peter 1:7)—a truth he does seem to know and acknowledges later on (Job 23:10; see Week 8, Day 4). His friends' persistent badgering that only the wicked suffer is making things worse.

Where do you see yourself in this? Can you identify with Job in any way? How is your relationship with God? What is your understanding of Him, of His ways? Does God treat the guiltless the same way He treats the guilty? How do grace and mercy fit into these simple models? Does God mingle mercy with His justice?

Romans 6:23 tells us that all have sinned and fallen short of the glory of God and therefore die because "the wages of sin is death." "There is none righteous, not one"

(Romans 3:10). But God in His mercy has provided a way for us to escape His just sentence of eternal death. We can't pay the penalty to escape, but God sent His Son, Jesus—who knew no sin—to die for us on the cross, to pay the price we cannot pay. He overcame death through a resurrection that guarantees that He will save those who believe in Him—in *His* death, *His* burial, *His* resurrection, and *His* atonement for sin. He will save them from eternal death and give them eternal life. On the basis of these facts alone we can have a secure hope and not despair. We don't need to have all the answers in our temporal world—not when we know that God loved us enough to provide a way into His eternal home.

REPENT!

Do you recognize sin in your life? Knowing you are forgiven should not entice you to gloss over or ignore sins. God calls us to acknowledge, confess, and repent from sin. John wrote:

> If we confess our sins, He is faithful and righteous to forgive us our sins and to cleanse us from all unrighteousness. If we say that we have not sinned, we make Him a liar, and His word is not in us (1 John 1:9-10).

Job's friends believed his suffering was due to unconfessed sin. Therefore, if Job would just repent, his suffering would end. "Confess and repent!" they tell him throughout the book.

DAY ONE

Read Job 11 and mark key words and phrases. In this chapter and chapters 12–14, mark *wisdom*[3] as one of the key words.

In this chapter, Job's third friend, Zophar, tries to help Job understand his plight and to recommend a solution just as the other two friends have done.

DAY TWO

Look at Zophar's argument in Job 11 again today. Write down the main points and see what you think is his most important one. Observe the tone of his words. Is he compassionate or harsh?

Also be sure to list what you learn about God from what Zophar says. What characteristics of God does he appeal to in his argument?

How does Zophar describe Job?

Be sure to add the theme of Job 11 to JOB AT A GLANCE.

DAY THREE

In chapters 12–14 Job responds to Zophar's demand that he repent. Today read Job 12, marking key words and phrases from your bookmark and noting the key elements in Job's reasoning.

Don't forget to add the theme of chapter 12 to JOB AT A GLANCE.

DAY FOUR

Read Job 13 and mark the key words and phrases from your bookmark.

Don't forget to add the theme of chapter 13 to JOB AT A GLANCE.

DAY FIVE

Read and mark Job 14 today. This chapter completes Job's response to Zophar's counsel that he repent of the sin he's hiding.

Don't forget to add the theme of chapter 14 to JOB AT A GLANCE.

DAY SIX

Make an outline of Zophar's charge and Job's response. Be sure you follow each point and counterpoint they make, remembering that God will conclude that Job's friends misrepresent Him. Zophar appeals to true characteristics of God, but does he misapply them? Is Job still caught up in despair? Is his argument fully or only partly true?

These chapters end the first "cycle" of discourses by Job and his friends. Job speaks first and then each of his friends speak and Job responds. If you've been filling out JOB AT A GLANCE faithfully, you can also mark these chapters as a segment. You might also mark the chapters and color-code them by the main speaker. JOB AT A GLANCE should show you the flow of thought so far in Job. See if the chapter themes you've recorded give you the main gist of the arguments that have been made.

DAY SEVEN

Store in your heart: Job 13:15.

Read and discuss: Job 11:13-20; 12:1-6; 13:1-8,15-16; 14:15-20.

QUESTIONS FOR DISCUSSION OR INDIVIDUAL STUDY

∾ Discuss Zophar's argument and accusation. What is his main point?

∾ If you were counseling someone who was suffering, would you take Zophar's approach? How does he behave toward Job? What does he call him?

∾ Review Job's response using verses listed above. How does Job react to Zophar? What does he think about Zophar's claims?

∾ What does Job declare about his relationship to the Lord? What is the one thing God has not done to him? What does Job say he would do even if God killed him?

∾ Job has confidence in his integrity and hope in God, but does he continue to argue with God? What does this indicate about Job and his understanding of his circumstances?

∾ What do Job's friends say about God in the first 14 chapters?

∾ What have you learned about God so far in your study? Has this impacted your life in any way?

THOUGHT FOR THE WEEK

The place of repentance in the Christian life is often misunderstood. For ten chapters, we have seen the basic charge that Job is guilty of some secret sin, that his suffering is proof of that sin—the direct result of it—and that if Job will simply quit complaining and repent, God will bring him relief.

The three friends rightfully claim that no man is sinless. Job doesn't claim that he is sinless, but he does claim that he has done no sin that corresponds with this particular suffering.

The word *repent* is actually used only in Job 42:6. In the New Testament, repentance is almost always that "change of mind" that leads to salvation, an exchanging of beliefs from lies to true propositions about who God is and what He does. Similarly, the word *confession* in the New Testament usually refers to the declaration of truths God has revealed about Himself.

But the point Job's friends make, and one of the main points of the Epistle of 1 John, is that we must recognize our sin, agreeing with God that it is sin. God forgives the penalty of sin—all sin, past, present, and future—when we believe in Christ and are saved. But 1 John teaches us that we must be aware of the sin we continue to commit as we live out our imperfect lives. When we sin, we must see it as God sees it. Then He works in us to cleanse us. His verdict, "Not guilty in Christ," is based on Christ's finished work on the cross.

What is crucial to see in both the Old and New Testaments is that suffering does not end just because we repent and confess sin. Eliphaz, Bildad, and Zophar were wrong.

Your Own Mouth Condemns You

The second cycle begins. Eliphaz, Bildad, and Zophar take up new arguments against Job. Their assumptions haven't changed, only their approach: They strengthen the intensity of their argument that Job's undisclosed sin is causing his suffering. Job continues to effectively show that their argument is false. He knows his conscience is clean and his friends are misrepresenting God by equating affliction with punishment.

DAY ONE

Read Job 15 and mark key words and phrases. This chapter is the start of a new segment, the second cycle of discourses by Job and his friends, beginning again with Eliphaz.

Don't forget to add the theme of Job 15 to JOB AT A GLANCE.

DAY TWO

Watch Eliphaz' new approach. Eliphaz is now responding to Job's answer to his original accusation in Job 4 and

5, so you may want to quickly review your notes on those chapters and Job's first response. What is the main point Eliphaz is making in Job 15? Is he still basing his response on his own experience?

DAY THREE

Read Job 16. Continue marking key words and phrases from your bookmark as you have done in the past. This is the first of two chapters in which Job answers Eliphaz. Remember to list the main points of his response.

DAY FOUR

Compare Job's argument in Job 16 with Eliphaz' argument in Job 15. What does Eliphaz charge Job with? Watch how Job counters Eliphaz. Note Job's addresses to Eliphaz, his comments about God, and his description of his situation.

List the main points and counterpoints.

DAY FIVE

Read and mark Job 17, which concludes Job's response to Eliphaz' charges. In Job 16, Job said that his friends were "sorry comforters." What does he call these friends now?

DAY SIX

In two columns, list what Job says about himself and about God in Job 17. Where is his focus now?

Add the themes of Job 16 and 17 to the chart, JOB AT A GLANCE.

DAY SEVEN

Store in your heart: Job 16:21.

Read and discuss: Job 15:1-9,17-25; 16:1-5,16-17, 20; 17:1-2,6-10.

QUESTIONS FOR DISCUSSION OR INDIVIDUAL STUDY

∾ What does Eliphaz accuse Job of?

∾ What does Eliphaz mean when he says Job's own mouth condemns him?

∾ Eliphaz appealed to his own experience and a vision in his first discourse. What does he appeal to now?

∾ What does Eliphaz claim is true about the wicked (including Job)?

∾ How does Job respond? What does he say about what Eliphaz is saying?

∾ Considering Job's plight and Eliphaz' approach, do you think Eliphaz is being successful? Is he helping Job? What lesson can you draw for yourself regarding counseling people who are suffering?

∾ Describe Job's emotions. Have they changed since chapter 3?

∾ What have you learned about Job so far in this study? Is any of this applicable to your own life?

THOUGHT FOR THE WEEK

As the second cycle of discourse begins, not much has changed. Job's suffering is no less intense. His children, servants, and livestock are still gone, and he still has a disease that wracks him with pain. His hardened and runny skin is covered with sore boils, worms, and a crust of dirt; his eyes are dim from grief; his arms and legs are shadows; and his bones are clinging to his skin, which burns with fever.

His friends continue to tell him the sufferings are his fault—he has sinned and refuses to repent, so no relief is in sight. Repentance is the only solution they envision because they are blinded by the false notion that only the wicked are afflicted. They even claim that those who protest their innocence the strongest are the most guilty.

Where is compassion? Where is comfort? The words become more harsh and strident as we move on. The friends' insistence that Job agree with them becomes stronger too.

Paul wrote to the Corinthian church that God is the God of all comfort and that He comforts us so that we might minister comfort to others. Jesus was afflicted so He might comfort us; Paul was afflicted so he could comfort the Corinthians. The principle is clear: Our afflictions are a platform from which we can comfort others who are afflicted.

One lesson we can take from the book of Job is that the proposition "Only sinners suffer" is not true and can't extend comfort to people who are suffering. It didn't console Job, and it won't console anyone we know, including ourselves. Nothing in this statement fully explains suffering or even approximates the teachings of Scripture on comfort, consolation, condolence, and compassion.

How will you help your friends? How do you want them to comfort you when you're afflicted? What principles, what precepts of life have you gained that will enable you to minister to others?

ADDING INSULT
TO INJURY

As the second cycle of discourse ends, Bildad and Zophar again address Job, and Job again responds. The two appear to have lost some of the patience they had in the first cycle, not only with Job but also with each other. One accuses the other of thinking like a beast. Words have become tools to wound with—as if Job's pain were not deep enough.

DAY ONE

Read and mark Job 18 according to the bookmark you have been using. Note the list of what happens to the wicked. How does this parallel what happened to Job in the first two chapters? What is Bildad's point?

Record the theme of Job 18 on JOB AT A GLANCE.

DAY TWO

Read Job 19 today, continuing to mark as you have before. Notice the relationship between Job 18 and 19. Also note the things Job says about God and others—brothers, family, and friends. Pay special attention to verse 25.

Don't forget to add the theme of Job 19 to JOB AT A GLANCE.

DAY THREE

Review the exchange between Bildad and Job in chapters 18 and 19—the second one between them. How would you characterize this exchange? Are any new points added to the exchange in chapters 8–10? Try listing the points in both exchanges so you can observe the similarities and differences, especially regarding suffering and sin.

DAY FOUR

Read and mark Job 20 and then record the theme on JOB AT A GLANCE. Zophar's address concerns what God does to whom? List what Zophar claims God does to the wicked and any parallels to Job 1 and 2.

DAY FIVE

Read Job 21, marking those things listed on your bookmark. Summarize the theme of Job 21 and record it on JOB AT A GLANCE.

DAY SIX

Review what Zophar and Job have said to one another in Job 20–21. What did Zophar appeal to in his first discourse in chapter 11? Now what does he appeal to? Contrast the two speeches by listing the main points in two columns. Then look at Job's responses to both and see what similarities you observe.

DAY SEVEN

 Store in your heart: Job 19:25.
Read and discuss: Job 19:23-29; 20:1-11; 21:1-26.

QUESTIONS FOR DISCUSSION OR INDIVIDUAL STUDY

∽ Review Bildad's main argument in this discourse.

∽ How does Job answer? What does he mean when he says he has been insulted ten times? (There have been only five speeches from friends to this point.)

∽ Why does Job feel insulted?

∽ Why does Job talk about his Redeemer? What has been the basic charge from his friends?

∽ What new tactic does Zophar try in this speech? How does it relate to Job's stated desire to die?

∽ When Job responds to Zophar, why does he say Zophar should be astonished and put his hand over his mouth? Can you see anything wrong with Zophar's reasoning? Does Job's response make more sense than Zophar's claim?

∽ What do you learn either positively or negatively from Bildad and Zophar as counselors/comforters?

∽ What insights can you gain about how we can slip into personal attacks rather than addressing the issue?

ᙖ Discuss some examples of how you might have acted like Bildad or Zophar or even Job, when provoked, and how you might do better the next time.

THOUGHT FOR THE WEEK

"As for me, I know that my Redeemer lives, and at the last He will take His stand on the earth" (Job 19:25). Wow! How can Job make this powerful theological statement? Isn't this a New Testament truth?

What does Job know about his Living Redeemer?

First, some words of introduction. The Hebrew word translated *Redeemer* is *Go-El*—the kinsman-redeemer written about in the Law and illustrated so beautifully in the book of Ruth. One of the roles of the kinsman-redeemer was to reclaim either the property of a relative or the relative himself by paying down debts the relative accrued by poverty. In Old Testament times, if a person didn't have property to satisfy debt claims, he could sell himself into slavery, hopefully temporarily. The kinsman-redeemer also avenged unlawful deaths of relatives. He was usually the closest blood relative willing and able to perform these tasks.

Job says his Redeemer lives and will take His stand on the earth "at the last." Surely Job is declaring that God is his Redeemer. As we study the theology of the kinsman-redeemer, we clearly see that Jesus fulfills this role for us. He took on flesh and blood so He would be a close relative. We were sold into slavery to sin by the fall of Adam, held under the dominion of him who had the power over death, Satan. Jesus paid the price of redemption: innocent blood. Only a perfectly sinless person could redeem the slaves of sin. Jesus alone had the assets to pay, and He was most willing.

And Jesus lives! He rose from the dead, and the disciples and more than 500 additional believers witnessed His resurrection. Many of these were alive when Paul wrote to the Corinthian church about the resurrection. Jesus ascended into heaven and sits at the right hand of the Father, and He will one day return to judge the living and the dead. Then He will take His stand on the earth—"at the last."

What a marvelous Messianic prophecy this is—"My redeemer lives!" If Job lived roughly in the time of Abraham (this is not certain), his declaration in Job 19:25 ranks with Genesis 3:15 and 15:6 as the earliest and most powerful declarations of the Gospel—a promised seed of Adam to crush Satan's head, a promised seed of Abraham in whom we must believe for righteousness (Galatians 3:16 shows that this is Jesus), and a Redeemer who lives and who will take His stand on the earth "at the last."

Who would have known that Job knew about the promised Messiah who redeems us from sin and its consequences? John wrote in Revelation 21:4, "And He will wipe away every tear from their eyes; and there will no longer be any death; there will no longer be any mourning, or crying, or pain; the first things have passed away."

Come quickly, Lord Jesus!

THE ALMIGHTY WILL BE YOUR GOLD

"Place your gold in the dust ... among the stones of the brooks, then the Almighty will be your gold and choice silver to you" (Job 22:24-25). Here, Eliphaz counsels Job to exchange objects of faith—exchange golds. He assumes Job is still trusting in wealth and is depressed either because of the wealth he has lost or because he has a few valuables remaining (possibly some gold) to which he's clinging. To Eliphaz, Job needs to address this compromised faith in God.

Is Eliphaz' assumption correct? Is Job's focus on gold, or is he completely absorbed in some other idea, such as one of God's attributes? Which one? Does Job believe God is Almighty? How about just? Is the object of his faith wealth or something else? What's really dismaying him? What does he say? What would you do in his circumstances?

DAY ONE

Read Job 22, the speech of Eliphaz in the third cycle of discourses. Mark words and phrases from your bookmark and note the main points of Eliphaz' charge to Job.

DAY TWO

Eliphaz seems to accuse Job of trusting in wealth rather than in God. The New Testament speaks to the same subject. Read Matthew 6:19-21; Mark 10:17-22; Luke 12:34; and Revelation 3:14-18. Summarize what relationships we should have with earthly riches and heavenly riches. What parallel do you see with the idea Eliphaz is using?

Add the theme of Job 22 to JOB AT A GLANCE.

DAY THREE

Read Job 23 today, marking as you have before. This is the first of two chapters that give Job's response to Eliphaz.

DAY FOUR

Read Job 23:10. Job now reveals that he understands the concept of refining believers, though earlier his perspective on suffering seemed to preclude this possibility. Read the following Scriptures that speak of refining: Psalm 12:6; Psalm 66:10; Proverbs 17:3; Isaiah 48:10; Jeremiah 9:7; Zechariah 13:9. Note who refines, who or what is refined, and how the refining is done. Do you think refining is always pleasant?

Add the theme of Job 23 to JOB AT A GLANCE.

DAY FIVE

Read Job 24, marking as you have before, using your bookmark. Watch the context carefully to differentiate the wicked from their victims. "They" are not all wicked.

DAY SIX

Eliphaz continues to insist that only the wicked suffer, that God punishes only them. In previous chapters, Job said that the wicked do not always suffer. They seem to get away with things. List what Job says in this chapter that wicked people do and what happens to them. Then compare what Job has said about the wicked in Job 9:22-24; 10:1-3; 21:7.

Add the theme of Job 24 to JOB AT A GLANCE.

DAY SEVEN

 Store in your heart: Job 23:10.
Read and discuss: Job 22:1-11, 21-30; 23:1-3, 8-17.

QUESTIONS FOR DISCUSSION OR INDIVIDUAL STUDY

- What charge does Eliphaz bring against Job in Job 22:6-9? List the specific sins Eliphaz charges Job has committed.

- What actions does Eliphaz demand Job take because of these sins?

∽ Eliphaz states that Job should not trust in his wealth but in God, who is true wealth. How do the cross-references you looked at agree or disagree with this?

∽ Does Job agree with Eliphaz?

∽ What does Job say God is doing through these afflictions? Is this view consistent with Scripture?

∽ Does Job still maintain a high view of God? Can you list what Job says about God that shows his reverence, fear, or awe of God?

∽ To what extent do you trust in wealth or riches of this earth? Can you really say you trust God? (Be careful— this one might hurt!)

∽ What is your view of God? Do you revere Him? Are you in awe of Him? Why do you have this view?

THOUGHT FOR THE WEEK

The physical process of refining is common. Crude oil is refined into fuels and lubricants. Foodstuffs like sugar and flour are refined. In every case, refining is intended to make products more useful and beneficial.

In Scripture, the principal objects of refining are silver and gold. The metal is placed in a crucible over an intense fire. The refiner increases the heat, bringing impurities to the surface. He then skims off this "dross," turns the heat up again, and repeats the process until he can see his reflection in the pure metal.

This process is frequently used in Scripture metaphorically for the refining of believers—the purging out of their sins. God refines us, testing our hearts in furnaces of affliction (see Deuteronomy 4:20). Job knew that he would come through this fire as gold. He knew the fire he was in was not intended for punishment even though his three friends disagreed.

This can be our situation too. We can know that we are righteous in the eyes of God because we believe the Gospel, and He has justified us by faith in the perfect life and death of Jesus Christ. We can know that God will refine us as gold, purging out our residual sin. But we must also heed what God says about the riches of earth and the riches of heaven. If we continue to trust in this world's wealth rather than God, we will not come through testing as pure gold.

Job's friends continued to claim that Job's suffering was a result of some specific sin or sins and that he could end his afflictions by repenting, but Job knew that God uses affliction to test the integrity of hearts and that pure hearts can stand the tests.

What about you? Do you have this confidence Job had? Do you store treasures in heaven that are imperishable and cannot be burned up? When affliction comes, will you pass the test and come through these trials refined as silver or gold?

THE FEAR OF THE LORD, THAT IS WISDOM

Can true wisdom be mined from the earth in gold, silver, or precious jewels? Do the creatures of the air, land, or sea possess wisdom or can they help us find it? Is wisdom found in education, degrees, or diplomas? Or is wisdom found only in God?

DAY ONE

Read Job 25, marking as you have before. This is the discourse of Bildad in the third cycle of discourses. This short chapter contains one readily apparent point. Record the theme of Job 25 in JOB AT A GLANCE.

DAY TWO

Read and mark Job 26 using your bookmark to help you. Job 26 begins Job's six-chapter response to Bildad.

DAY THREE

Did you sense the sarcasm in Job's response to Bildad? Reread Job 26:1-4. These discourses are supposed to be point/counterpoint—one party claims something, and then the other refutes it. At this point, however, what is Job doing?

From Job 26:5-15, make a list of examples of God's sovereignty. Then consider the relationship of Job 26:1-4 to Job 26:5-15 in light of Bildad's charge against Job in chapter 25. What is Job's main point about God?

Record the theme of Job 26 on JOB AT A GLANCE.

DAY FOUR

Read Job 27, marking key words and phrases on your bookmark.

DAY FIVE

List the faith actions in Job 27 that Job plans to do in spite of his circumstances. Then make a list of God's judgments on the wicked—their "inheritance" from Him (27:13). Why does Job make these two distinctions? Think about Bildad's charge (also Eliphaz' and Zophar's) throughout Job. Then add the theme of Job 27 to JOB AT A GLANCE.

DAY SIX

Today read and mark Job 28—a continuation of chapter 27. Don't miss *wisdom*. When you finish, consider how this fits with Job 27. Does Job speak of the wicked or the righteous man? Record the theme of Job 28 on JOB AT A GLANCE.

DAY SEVEN

Store in your heart: Job 28:28.

Read and discuss: Job 25:1-6; 26:1-4; 27:1-12, 23; 28:12-20, 28.

QUESTIONS FOR DISCUSSION OR INDIVIDUAL STUDY

∾ What charge does Bildad bring against Job in chapter 25?

∾ How does Job respond? Does he respond directly to Bildad's words or to his method?

∾ How tempting is responding to an antagonist the way Job does? Do you find that exasperation sometimes causes people to make personal attacks rather than "sticking with the facts"? Can you think of any examples of this?

∾ What view does Job have of God? Is your view like Job's? Why?

∾ What does Job say he will do toward God even though God afflicts him? Can you say this too? Why?

∾ Discuss what Job says is the portion (inheritance) of the wicked. In light of the accusations his friends make, why does he give this description of the wicked's portion?

∾ According to Job 28, where is wisdom found and where is it not found?

∾ Where should one look for wisdom? Is it found in the creation or in the Creator?

THOUGHT FOR THE WEEK

Despite the technological marvels of the past 100 years—all that mankind has discovered and invented—nothing on earth can show us true wisdom.

We cannot dig in a mine to find wisdom. We cannot find it from the animals that inhabit the earth; none of them can say, "Here is wisdom." We cannot even find it in the writings of men, who can record only the thoughts of men. Although most people look to the great intellectuals for wisdom, what they find instead are theories—ideas and speculations about what they don't know.

No! Wisdom comes from the fear of God!

People who do not fear God can never find wisdom because wisdom comes from God. Proverbs 2:6-7 says, "For the LORD gives wisdom; from His mouth come knowledge and understanding. He stores up sound wisdom for the upright." Proverbs 9:10 says, "The fear of the LORD is the beginning of wisdom, and the knowledge of the Holy One is understanding."

What is the fear of God? The Hebrew word translated by the English word "fear" when we read "fear of God" in the Bible means respect, awe, or reverence. If you fear God, you have a respect for God's authority and power, His right to judge; you are in awe of His holiness and justice, and you live with a reverence for God—who He is and what He has done and will do for you.

How foolish we are to look elsewhere. How foolish we are to trust in the words of those who do not know God. Yes, such people may acquire knowledge of history or mathematics or science, but they know nothing of the mystery of wickedness, the fate of the wicked, or the hope of the righteous. They don't know what love, justice, and mercy are, and they have no knowledge of the Living God. They have no understanding and no wisdom because these are gifts God gives to His people alone. Paul wrote to the Corinthian church about the great contrast between the wisdom of the world and God's wisdom, and that Christ became God's wisdom to us (1 Corinthians 1:18-31).

Those in Christ are not "wise according to the flesh," as men judge wisdom (1 Corinthians 1:26). But we must never forget that true wisdom comes only from God and that the beginning of wisdom is the fear of God.

THE GOOD OLD DAYS

When life seems very difficult, we sometimes escape pain by fantasizing about "the good old days." Longing to be in a time when life was good—when we enjoyed better health and happier relationships—we try to mentally escape the pain and struggle of today's circumstances. We sometimes dress up the memories better than the facts, forgetting or deliberately ignoring the difficulties we had in those days, pretending instead that the circumstances were ideal. Is this the best for us? Let's see if Job has any regrets as he reflects on his "good old days."

DAY ONE

Read and mark Job 29 using your bookmark as you have before. This chapter continues Job's response to Bildad that began in Job 26.

DAY TWO

List some items from Job's assessment of his life before he lost his family, possessions, and health, but don't rewrite the chapter. Making the list will help you see how Job saw himself before calamity struck.

Now record the theme of Job 29 on JOB AT A GLANCE.

DAY THREE

Today read Job 30, marking key words and phrases.

DAY FOUR

List what Job says about how others see him and act toward him. Then list how Job sees himself. Lastly, list what Job says about his relationship to God.

Don't forget to record the theme of Job 30 on JOB AT A GLANCE.

DAY FIVE

Read Job 31, marking key words and phrases. Notice the repetition of *if.* You might want to mark *if* in this chapter to help you see the flow of thought.

DAY SIX

Make a list of things Job says he might have done. In a parallel list, show what he says God should do. In this list, think about what Job is doing with regard to sin. As usual, list what you learn about God in this chapter. Then add the theme of Job 31 to JOB AT A GLANCE.

DAY SEVEN

Store in your heart: Job 31:1.

Read and discuss: Job 29:1-10,21-25; 30:1,9-11, 15-16,20-23,26-31; 31:1-6,24-28.

QUESTIONS FOR DISCUSSION OR INDIVIDUAL STUDY

∽ What is Job's desire in chapter 29?

∽ Have you ever felt this way? What do you think about Job's thinking, and what do you think about yourself when you indulge in this kind of thinking?

∽ Discuss how Job sees his present condition in chapter 30.

∽ What does Job say about how others see him?

∽ How does Job describe his relationship to God in Job 30?

∽ What is Job doing or saying in Job 31? Discuss the various kinds of sins he lists.

∽ What is Job's view of God and of his own sin? Should God judge sin?

∽ Does Job really think he has done all these sins, or is he simply declaring righteous judgments for them?

∽ After Job cries out all these things, what response is he looking for? From whom?

∽ What lessons can we learn from Job in chapter 31? Should we not only confess sin to God but also agree that He should judge our sin?

THOUGHT FOR THE WEEK

In Genesis 18:25 Abraham asked, "Shall not the judge of all the earth deal justly?" Our understanding of God's attitude toward sin helps determine the way we view ourselves and our circumstances.

Rarely today do we hear anything about God's righteous judgments on sin. Those who speak such things are considered "wild-eyed, crazy, Bible-thumping fundamentalists" and "reactionary, right-wing Christians." What people want to hear is that God loves them and has forgiven them.

Christians and non-Christians alike sometimes focus on memories of good times to escape the drudgery of everyday life and the pain and heartache of broken relationships. But God does not call us to think this way, to live in the past. What God calls us to do is to run to Him—now!

God has paid the price for our sins by sending His Son, Jesus, to die on the cross in our place. If we believe the Gospel, God forgives the debt we've accrued and doesn't require us to suffer the just penalty of eternal death. But this does not mean that we do not suffer any consequences from sin. Certainly, hiding in a fantasy world of happy memories does not help us become the mature believers God wants us to be. He wants us to know that He alone is our refuge, He alone is our comfort, He alone is the One who can lift us up from despair, pain, and suffering. When you have lost everything, you still have God. He alone has the power to rescue you.

Life is hard. Physical pain, illness, suffering, and death abound—all consequences of the first sin of Adam. Non-biblical answers to these problems are distortions of the truth by our adversary, Satan. This is how Satan operates: He distorts truth, and we are tempted to believe him rather than God.

That's why we must always remember that what God does is always just, always good, always right, always best for us. We must always cling to the truth that nothing can separate us from the love of God. We must always cry out to God in our affliction not only because He is our hope but also because the cry itself is an act of worship, showing that we place Him above all else.

The truly good days lie not in the past but in the future. The lure of "the good old days" is really part of Satan's attempt to divert our eyes from the hope of our presence with the Lord in eternity—perpetual worship without pain or tears. Don't wish for the past but for the future, which will be better than anything you have ever experienced or can imagine.

GOD DOES NO WRONG

Why do we trust someone? Our confidence is based on his or her character. We don't trust a character marked with lying and deceitfulness. Why should we trust God? What is His character like? How can we hope in what God will do if we can't trust Him? And how can we trust Him if we don't know His character?

DAY ONE

Job 32 through 37 is the speech of a friend who has not spoken until now. We've read what Eliphaz, Bildad, and Zophar have said to Job, but now a new voice rises: Elihu's. This first chapter of his speech describes his relationship to the others and explains why he speaks now. Pay careful attention so that you will know who is speaking and who is listening as you read Job 32, marking as you have before. You might want to mark speaker and listener, but don't clutter up your page.

We're going to cover this speech in one week, so summarize Job 32 and record the theme on JOB AT A GLANCE.

DAY TWO

Read and mark Job 33 today using your bookmark to help you. Elihu addresses Job in this chapter. Watch what he says about God's relationship with Job and the flaws he sees in Job's arguments. Just for this chapter, mark *pit*. This will help you see the main argument Elihu makes. Don't forget to add to your list of God's characteristics. Which characteristic keeps people from the pit?

Record the theme of Job 33 on JOB AT A GLANCE.

DAY THREE

Elihu turns again to Job's friends in Job 34. Mark key words and phrases in Job 34 as usual. Note the main points about God and what Bildad, Eliphaz, and Zophar say about God and Job.

Remember to summarize the theme of Job 34 and record it on JOB AT A GLANCE.

DAY FOUR

Read Job 35, marking key words and phrases on your bookmark. Note whom Elihu is addressing and what he says about God. Record the theme of Job 35 on JOB AT A GLANCE.

DAY FIVE

Read and mark Job 36 today. You should add much in this chapter to the list about God you've been making these past weeks.

Then add the theme of Job 36 to JOB AT A GLANCE.

DAY SIX

Today read and mark Job 37, the end of Elihu's speech. As Elihu says to Job, consider the wonders of God in this chapter. Add them to your list about God.

Then record the theme of Job 37 on JOB AT A GLANCE.

DAY SEVEN

 Store in your heart: Job 34:12.

Read and discuss: Job 32:11-22; 33:8-18; 34:1-13; 35:13-16; 36:5-7,17-18; 37:14,23-24.

QUESTIONS FOR DISCUSSION OR INDIVIDUAL STUDY

- Discuss who is speaking and what his relationships are to the characters we have seen in Job thus far.

- What is his intention in this speech? Whom does he address?

∾ As he begins his actual speech in Job 33, whom is he addressing, and what charge does he bring? What is the basis of his argument that Job is wrong?

∾ Whom does Elihu address in Job 34? What charge does he bring, and what is the basis of his argument?

∾ Discuss whom Elihu addresses in Job 35 and what his main points are. Notice that the beginning of Job 35 is a continuation of Job 34:34. What is the main point?

∾ Discuss what you learn about God from these chapters.

∾ Previously, Job's friends had argued that what had happened to him was God's just judgment on sin. What characteristic of God does Elihu now bring to the table? Discuss what you learn about God and "the pit."

THOUGHT FOR THE WEEK

Understanding the character of God is key to understanding God's ways. God never acts in ways that are contradictory to His character. In the speeches of Job and all four of his friends, the central issue is, Why is Job suffering? All four friends offer an explanation based on their understanding of God's character and His ways. However, in Job 42:7 God says to three of them—Eliphaz, Bildad, and Zophar—"You have not spoken of Me what is right as My servant Job has."

Because these three had not understood God's character, they misrepresented Him to Job. For this reason, God's wrath burned against them. Not every Bible teacher or preacher properly represents God. If you do not know what God says about Himself in His Word, you can easily believe a lie. This is why we urge every believer to study God's Word inductively—to see what God Himself says.

God's attributes and character cannot be fully described in just a few words. The book of Job has taught us that God is omniscient. We should also know from this book that God is omnipotent. He has power over all creation—nature, man, the angelic realm, Satan himself. And we should know that God is just in all His ways.

But how do we apply such things practically? How can we take things we see on paper and translate them into life? Understanding must translate into living.

Job 28:28 tells us, "The fear of the Lord, that is wisdom; and to depart from evil is understanding." Similarly, Psalm 111:10 tells us, "The fear of the LORD is the beginning of wisdom; a good understanding have all those who do His commandments." These are not just concepts but also life-changing actions. Departing from evil begins as a concept—we can think about it—but it must become an action, the action of obedience. Both influence the way we live moment by moment: God wants us to think and do right. More than a dozen proverbs speak of the fear of the Lord and God's wisdom, a wisdom that teaches us to walk correctly.

What does *the fear of the Lord* mean? The Hebrew word captures the ordinary sense of being afraid of something, but its persistent connection with wisdom requires a more complex sense, something beyond a simple "shrinking away from." We reverence things we're in awe of. Accordingly, we understand *the fear of the Lord* as a reverential fear, and this is the way it should be because the character of God is, in fact, very awesome. What God knows and does is awesome compared to what we know and do. We're commanded to fear the Lord (Deuteronomy 10:20), so we *ought* to fear Him, to be awed by Him, to revere Him. This is a healthy sense of fear—one that is good for us.

We are right to understand God's judgments in a reverential way because He is Judge. Sinners rightfully fear God's wrath because His wrath is greater than man's. If He created the universe, He can destroy it. What is man compared to this?

So then, how should we live before God if He knows all we think and sees all we do? Are any of us without sin? Without blame? Meditate on what 1 John 1:8-10 teaches us about our sin:

> If we say that we have no sin, we are deceiving ourselves and the truth is not in us. If we confess our sins, He is faithful and righteous to forgive us our sins and to cleanse us from all unrighteousness. If we say that we have not sinned, we make Him a liar and His word is not in us (1 John 1:8-10).

We cannot be perfect, but how then should we live?

WILL THE FAULTFINDER CONTEND WITH THE ALMIGHTY?

When Abraham was 99 years old, God appeared to him and said, "I am *El Shaddai,* God Almighty; walk before Me and be blameless." God then opened Sarah's womb when she was 89 years old and gave her a child. Job uses the word *Almighty* 31 times, more than half the uses in the Bible. If we learn anything at all about God in Job, we learn that He is Almighty.

DAY ONE

Read Job 38, marking as you have before. This begins God's response to all that has been said thus far. Don't miss *wisdom.*

DAY TWO

Make a list of things God can do that man can't. Can you see that He is God Almighty?

Record the theme of Job 38 on JOB AT A GLANCE.

DAY THREE

Read and mark Job 39. Again, don't miss *wisdom.*

DAY FOUR

Even though you did not mark *God* often, this chapter is filled with truth about Him. So continue your list of what God can do and man can't.

Record the theme of Job 39 on JOB AT A GLANCE.

DAY FIVE

Read Job 40. Mark key words and phrases as you have before.

DAY SIX

Continue listing what God can do that man can't. Also note that Job briefly answers God in this chapter. Then record the theme of Job 40 on JOB AT A GLANCE.

DAY SEVEN

 Store in your heart: Job 40:2.
Read and discuss: Job 38:1-7; 40:1-9.

QUESTIONS FOR DISCUSSION OR INDIVIDUAL STUDY

∾ Discuss what God says He can do that man can't. This may take some time because the list is long, but the information deserves thorough discussion.

∾ How does Job respond to God?

∾ What view does Job have of God?

WEEK TWELVE 89

- Why does God say all these things? Why the long list?

- In reviewing all that God says He can do, do you, like Job, feel insignificant in comparison to His power? Are you beginning to have an understanding of God's omnipotence? How has God spoken to you this week in His Word?

THOUGHT FOR THE WEEK

Almighty God. The phrase is often used by people who do not even think about just *how* powerful God is or what *almighty* really means. All might. All power. The English word *all* is translated from the word Latin *omni,* and the English word *power* from the Latin word for "potent." So *omnipotent* simply combines the two Latin terms and is conceptually equivalent to "all-mighty" or "all-power."

These chapters give one of the most comprehensive descriptions of God's omnipotence in all of Scripture, but we can also look at the rest of Scripture for additional insight into God's power.

According to Genesis 1 and 2, God created the heavens and the earth and all that is on the earth. Notice some details in Job 38:1-38 that are not given in Genesis. The descriptions here are specific and completely understandable. Clouds are "water jars of heaven" pouring out rain so that dust hardens into a mass and clods stick together. These are practical descriptions of a power that is actually very difficult to understand.

We cannot understand *how* God made this all work together. Creation is beyond comprehension because we can't see, feel, hear, taste, or touch the whole of it, nor were we present when it was made by the invisible Creator. We can perceive, however, some *objects* that were created, like rain, and the *results of other objects,* like wind (we can't see the wind itself, but we can watch the tree bending).

God tells us that He controls everything in creation— He makes rain and He causes the wind to blow. These providences are things we can understand. The book of Job makes use of sensual images to explain creation and providence—what God has made and what He regulates. Man can neither create nor fully control nature.

God Himself is also beyond our comprehension. To explain Himself to us in terms we could understand, He promised a Messiah and then made His Word flesh (John 1:1-18). John 14:8-11 describes this beautifully. When Philip asks Jesus to "show" them the Father, Jesus replies that seeing Him was the same as seeing the Father. Jesus came to show us the Father in ways we could perceive with our minds. In a similar manner, He ate a fish and had Thomas touch His wounds so His disciples would realize He was not just a ghost after His resurrection.

Yet Jesus taught that those who believe apart from their physical senses are blessed: "Blessed are they who did not see, and yet believed" (John 20:29). God's essence is invisible (Colossians 1:15; 1 Timothy 1:17; Hebrews 11:27). Immutability, omnipotence, omniscience, and omnipresence cannot be seen, tasted, or touched. God's eternal nature cannot be heard or smelled. Man's limited mind is forced to rest on the clear, noncontradictory revelation God has given. This is faith!

Job's senses reported to him that his possessions had been destroyed, but his mind could not understand why.

We are much like Job. Our senses reveal pain, loss, and disaster to us, and our minds do not understand. We can't comprehend why these things happen.

What God asks of us is faith in Him during these times.

BUT NOW MY EYES
SEE YOU

"I have heard of You by the hearing of the ear, but now my eyes see You" (Job 42:5). Knowing by hearsay and knowing by sight are vastly different. In the former sense, God's Words go in one ear and out the other; in the latter, we actually see God acting in our lives. This wasn't an easy lesson for Job, but the result was beyond imagination. He died a richer man than before—not just richer in possessions and family, but richer in his relationship to God.

DAY ONE

Read Job 41, marking as you have before. This is the rest of God's response to the speeches of Eliphaz, Bildad, Zophar, Elihu, and Job.

DAY TWO

Continue adding to your list of what God can do and man can't. Also make a list of the characteristics of Leviathan.

Record the theme of Job 41 in JOB AT A GLANCE.

DAY THREE

Read and mark the final chapter, Job 42. After God's rebuke, Job responds. We have the climax and the end of the story.

DAY FOUR

List what Job says he has realized. Also list what the Lord says to Job's friends. Then list what the Lord does for Job. Record the theme of Job 42 on JOB AT A GLANCE.

DAY FIVE

Go back to Job 1 and list Job's possessions: the size of his family and the numbers associated with his properties. Then make a parallel list from Job 42 of what the Lord gives him. Also compare Job 42:11 and Job 2:11.

Think about what had happened in between. What do you learn about comfort and consolation?

Read Psalm 23:4; 86:17; 119:50,76; Isaiah 49:13; Jeremiah 31:13; Acts 9:31; 1 Corinthians 14:3; 2 Corinthians 1:3-7; 1 Thessalonians 4:18; and 2 Thessalonians 2:16-17.

List what the Bible teaches about consolation and comfort for those who are in distress.

DAY SIX

We have come to the end of our study. By now JOB AT A GLANCE has all 42 chapter themes on it. Add key words you marked, the purpose of the book, or any other things you have discerned. Lastly, write the theme of Job on the chart. Perhaps you can find a key verse or portion that sums up the message of the entire book. If so, use that. Remember, God hasn't revealed themes, but you can summarize what God has said.

Review all of Job. If you have time, read through all 42 chapters of Job and spend some time reflecting on what you learned. If time is at a premium, review JOB AT A GLANCE and reflect on all you have learned. Perhaps you would like to spend some time in prayer or praise to God for the wonder of His grace and goodness.

DAY SEVEN

 Store in your heart: Job 42:5.
Read and discuss: Job 42.

QUESTIONS FOR DISCUSSION OR INDIVIDUAL STUDY

- Discuss what Job had at the beginning and what he received at the end.

- Discuss what the Lord told Job's friends they needed to do. What would Job do? What would the Lord do?

- How did the Lord view these friends? How did He view Job?

- What view does Job have of God?

- What did you learn about comfort and consolation? Where are they found? What examples do we have from Job to help us comfort others?

- What did you learn from your study of Job about Satan and his relationship to God and to us?

❧ Share particular verses in Job that spoke to your heart—ones that you will remember.

❧ What do you think you will do when calamity strikes you or a friend or relative? How well will you respond? Has this study in Job prepared you to respond better to suffering and affliction?

THOUGHT FOR THE WEEK

Our three months studying Job together have passed quickly. Perhaps at times you were confused about what Job's friends were saying, unsure whether things they said were true or not. Remember, the best commentary on Scripture is Scripture itself. The study of God's entire Word helps us understand particular passages better. Misunderstanding God's Word is easy if we ignore this and other principles of study.

Job's friends misunderstood God. Job himself misunderstood God's ways, and so do we at times. But we should learn from Job to never lose faith in God even if we lose everything else. Keeping faith in such circumstances *is* possible. Job maintained an underlying confidence that his Redeemer would vindicate him in the end.

We can take heart in this final reward Job received for his faith. True, he received some rewards on earth but none that were immortal. His new children would die someday, as would his new cattle. And new children never replace old ones. The New Testament teaches us that the rewards in heaven are imperishable and everlasting. So Job's enduring faith can encourage and strengthen us. It can comfort and console us. It can give us hope when nothing else can because God is faithful.

We will all encounter great losses in our lives. Until the Lord takes us home, we will experience death of loved ones, friends, and relatives. Spouses, sons, and daughters may die before us. The pain of such losses is unimaginable. But a firm grip on God will strengthen us in times of loss. That is what the book of Job teaches. God is greater than man. He has created all things, and all things in heaven and earth are His. Our possessions are from God and belong to Him, and we are to be faithful stewards. Whatever He takes away is still His. We are simply no longer stewards of it.

This thought, like the hope of resurrection and being united with loved ones, can lessen the pain of losses: We do not grieve, Paul says, "as do the rest who have no hope" (1 Thessalonians 4:13). Losses put in the perspective of eternity are not the same as those in a life with no meaning. We don't have to understand why losses come. (They seldom have only one purpose.) God never gave Job reasons for his suffering. He wanted Job to trust Him, to maintain faith regardless of circumstances and motives. If we trust God only when circumstances agree with our standards of justice, then we do not trust Him fully. But God calls us to trust Him fully, wholeheartedly, perfectly, with no reservations whatsoever!

Faith that hangs on comprehension is not faith at all. God calls us to believe what He has revealed, but He hasn't revealed everything: "The secret things belong to the LORD our God, but the things revealed belong to us and to our sons forever, that we may observe all the words of this law" (Deuteronomy 29:29).

Life and death are in His hands. God gives health and possessions and even children as gifts. Remember what Job learned about God's sovereignty over possessions. The following may be platitudes to some, but to men and women of faith they are practical, encouraging truths:

> Naked I came from my mother's womb, and naked I shall return there. The LORD gave and the LORD has taken away. Blessed be the name of the LORD (1:21).

> Shall we indeed accept good from God and not accept adversity? (2:10).

> Though He slay me, I will hope in Him (13:15).

> But it is still my consolation, and I rejoice in unsparing pain, that I have not denied the words of the Holy One (6:10).

After Job lost everything, he kept faith in God. That is the message of Job to us as we live our lives on this earth amid sickness, death, and disaster. The message is that we can trust God in times of these extreme adversities.

Our prayer is that this study of Job will strengthen your faith and help you in your times of distress to hold on to your faith in God, the Almighty, no matter what. Then you, like Job, can be a testimony of God's faithfulness to your friends, family, and generations to come.

Theme of Job:

SEGMENT DIVISIONS

		CHAPTER THEMES
		1
		2
		3
		4
		5
		6
		7
		8
		9
		10
		11
		12
		13
		14
		15
		16
		17
		18
		19
		20
		21

Author:

Date:

Purpose:

Key Words:

wisdom

sin (iniquity, transgression)

sons of God

righteous (right, righteousness)

SEGMENT DIVISIONS

			CHAPTER THEMES
			22
			23
			24
			25
			26
			27
			28
			29
			30
			31
			32
			33
			34
			35
			36
			37
			38
			39
			40
			41
			42

NOTES

1. NIV: angels
2. NIV: angels
3. NIV: victory; NKJV: prudence

NOTES FOR PERSONAL STUDY

NOTES FOR PERSONAL STUDY

NOTES FOR PERSONAL STUDY

NOTES FOR PERSONAL STUDY

Notes for Personal Study

BOOKS IN THE
NEW INDUCTIVE STUDY SERIES

∾∾∾∾∾

Teach Me Your Ways
Genesis, Exodus,
Leviticus, Numbers, Deuteronomy

Choosing Victory,
Overcoming Defeat
Joshua, Judges, Ruth

Desiring God's Own Heart
1 & 2 Samuel, 1 Chronicles

Walking Faithfully with God
1 & 2 Kings, 2 Chronicles

Overcoming Fear
and Discouragement
Ezra, Nehemiah, Esther

Trusting God
in Times of Adversity
Job

God's Answers for
Today's Problems
Proverbs

God's Blueprint
for Bible Prophecy
Daniel

Discovering the God
of Second Chances
Jonah, Joel, Amos, Obadiah

Finding Hope
When Life Seems Dark
Hosea, Micah, Nahum,
Habakkuk, Zephaniah

Opening the Windows
of Blessings
Haggai, Zechariah, Malachi

The Call to Follow Jesus
Luke

The God who Cares
and Knows You
John

The Holy Spirit
Unleashed in You
Acts

God's Answers for
Relationships and Passions
1 & 2 Corinthians

Free from Bondage
God's Way
Galatians, Ephesians

That I May Know Him
Philippians, Colossians

Standing Firm in
These Last Days
1 & 2 Thessalonians

Walking in Power,
Love, and Discipline
1 & 2 Timothy, Titus

Living with Discernment
in the End Times
1 & 2 Peter, Jude

God's Love Alive in You
1, 2, & 3 John,
Philemon, James

Behold, Jesus Is Coming!
Revelation

Harvest House Books by Kay Arthur

～～～～～

Discover the Bible for Yourself
God, Are You There?
God, I Need Your Comfort
God, Help Me Experience More of You
How to Study Your Bible
Israel, My Beloved
Lord, Teach Me to Pray in 28 Days
Lord, Teach Me to Study the Bible in 28 Days
A Marriage Without Regrets
A Marriage Without Regrets Study Guide
Speak to My Heart, God
With an Everlasting Love

Bibles

The New Inductive Study Bible (NASB)

～～～～～

Discover 4 Yourself® Inductive Bible Studies for Kids

God, What's Your Name?
How to Study Your Bible for Kids
Lord, Teach Me to Pray for Kids
God's Amazing Creation (Genesis 1–2)
Digging Up the Past (Genesis 3–11)
Abraham—God's Brave Explorer (Genesis 11–25)
Extreme Adventures with God (Isaac, Esau, and Jacob)
Joseph—God's Superhero (Genesis 37–50)
You're a Brave Man, Daniel (Daniel 1-6)
Fast-Forward to the Future (Daniel 7-12)
Wrong Way, Jonah! (Jonah)
Jesus in the Spotlight (John 1–11)
Jesus—Awesome Power, Awesome Love (John 11–16)
Jesus—To Eternity and Beyond! (John 17–21)
Boy, Have I Got Problems! (James)
Bible Prophecy for Kids (Revelation 1-7)
A Sneak Peek into the Future (Revelation 8-22)

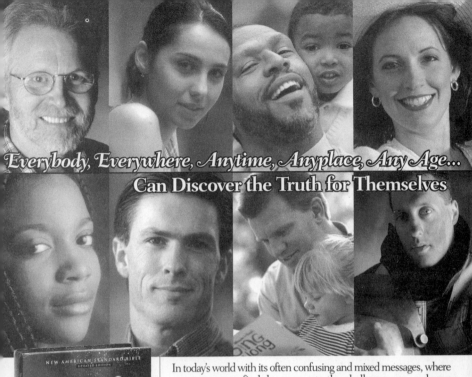

Everybody, Everywhere, Anytime, Anyplace, Any Age...
Can Discover the Truth for Themselves

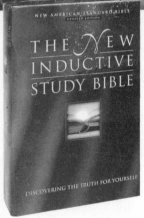

In today's world with its often confusing and mixed messages, where can you turn to find the answer to the challenges you and your family face? Whose word can you trust? Where can you turn when you need answers—about relationships, your children, your future?

The <u>Updated</u> New Inductive Study Bible

Open *this* study Bible and you will soon discover its uniqueness— unlike any other, this study Bible offers no notes, commentaries, or the opinions of others telling you what the Scripture is saying. It is in fact the only study Bible based entirely on the *inductive* study approach, providing you with instructions and the tools for observing what the text really says, interpreting what it means, and applying its principles to your life.

The only study Bible containing the *inductive study method* taught and endorsed by Kay Arthur and Precept Ministries.

• A new *smaller* size makes it easier to carry • individualized instructions for studying *every* book • guides for color marking keywords and themes • *Updated* NASB text • *improved* in-text maps and charts • 24 pages of full-color charts, historical timelines, & maps • self-discovery in its truest form

One Message, The Bible.
One Method, Inductive.

A SIMPLE, PROVEN APPROACH TO LETTING GOD'S WORD CHANGE YOUR LIFE...FOREVER

HARVEST HOUSE™
PUBLISHERS
EUGENE, OREGON

DIGGING DEEPER

❧❧❧❧

Books in the New Inductive Study Series are survey courses. If you want to do a more in-depth study of a particular book of the Bible, we suggest that you do a Precept Upon Precept Bible Study Course on that book. The Precept studies require approximately five hours of personal study a week. You may obtain more information on these powerful courses by contacting Precept Ministries International at 800-763-8280, visiting our website at www.precept.org, or filling out and mailing the response card in the back of this book.

If you desire to expand and sharpen your skills, you would really benefit by attending a Precept Ministries Institute of Training. The Institutes are conducted throughout the United States, Canada, and in a number of other countries. Class lengths vary from one to five days, depending on the course you are interested in. For more information on the Precept Ministries Institute of Training, call Precept Ministries.